Bev Aisbett is the author and illustrator of five highly regarded self-help texts for sufferers of anxiety and depression, most notably *Living with IT* and *Taming the Black Dog*. These books are distributed to health professionals nationwide and have been translated into four languages.

A trained counsellor, Bev is also the facilitator of the 'Working with IT' recovery program in Melbourne and assists those in other states through 'THE IT KIT', a home study version of the workshop. She conducts lectures to assist sufferers of depression and anxiety within metropolitan and regional Victoria.

Bev is also a recognised artist and her soulful paintings are regularly exhibited in Melbourne and Tasmania.

Workshop and lecture information: www.adavic.org
IT Kit information: www.bevaisbett.com

ALSO BY BEV AISBETT

The Book of IT

Fixing IT

Taming The Black Dog

Get Real

Letting IT Go

Living IT Up

Recovery: A Journey to Healing

The Little Book of IT

I
LOVE
ME

■HarperCollins*Publishers*

HarperCollins_Publishers_

First published in Australia in 2010
by HarperCollins_Publishers_ Australia Pty Limited
ABN 36 009 913 517
harpercollins.com.au

HarperCollins_Publishers_
25 Ryde Road, Pymble, Sydney, NSW 2073, Australia
31 View Road, Glenfield, Auckland 0627, New Zealand
A 53, Sector 57, Noida, UP, India
77–85 Fulham Palace Road, London, W6 8JB, United Kingdom
2 Bloor Street East, 20th floor, Toronto, Ontario M4W 1A8, Canada
10 East 53rd Street, New York NY 10022, USA

National Library of Australia Cataloguing-in-Publication data:

Aisbett, Bev.
     I love me/Bev Aisbett.
     ISBN 9780732289010 (pbk.).
     Depression, Mental. Stress (Psychology)
616.8527

Cover illustration by Bev Aisbett
Cover design by Christa Moffitt, Christabella Designs
Internal design by Ingrid Kwong
Typeset in 13pt Comic Sans
Printed and bound in Australia by Griffin Press
50gsm Bulky News used by HarperCollins_Publishers_ is a natural, recyclable product
made from wood grown in sustainable forests. The manufacturing processes conform
to the environmental regulations in the country of origin, New Zealand.

5 4 3   11 12 13

DEDICATION

To my beloved kelpie friend, Tao

For loyalty, comfort and seventeen years of the
kind of unconditional love I can only aspire to.

R.I.P. 30 March 2009

CONTENTS

INTRODUCTION   9

WHO DO YOU LOVE?
Overview   10

WHY CAN'T WE LOVE OURSELVES?
The fear of selfishness   20

I HATE ME
The origins of self-loathing   34

IT'S ALL ABOUT ME
The fear of change   52

ME AND MY SHADOW
Embracing the lost self   64

I FORGIVE ME
Forgiveness and self-love   78

I FORGIVE YOU
Forgiving others   90

LOVING ME, LOVING YOU
Self-worth in relationships   104

LOVE THE ONE YOU'RE WITH
Standing by yourself in tough times   122

ME, MYSELF AND I
The benefits of self-love   140

INTRODUCTION

Since 1992, when I first wrote *Living with IT*, I have been searching for the very heart of the malaise which affects not only those who suffer from anxiety and depression, but also human beings in general.

This malaise, which has become epidemic, manifests as anything from dissatisfaction to rage, bullying to brutality, self-pity to cynicism. It contaminates happiness, sabotages potential and saps joy. It renders its victims helpless and, once infected, their condition is extremely contagious. The disease is not discriminating: it infects world leaders and ordinary citizens alike.

What is this malaise? It is a lack of joy. It is existing instead of living, finding oneself empty and afraid, angry, full of blame or bored senseless. It is marrying the wrong spouse, staying in the job you hate, eating the wrong foods, becoming addicted, being lonely, falling ill, feeling lost.

But take heart. There is a cure which is free, powerful and accessible to all. It is lifesaving for wounded people.

Here it is: **LOVE YOURSELF**.

WHO DO YOU LOVE?

'God has entrusted me with myself'

Epictetus

Loving others.
It all seems very easy
and natural, doesn't it?

YOU'RE SO
BEAUTIFUL!

HOW'S MY
BEST GIRL?

YOU'RE A
GREAT PAL!

I LOVE
YOU!

We usually have no
problem telling others
who are dear to us that
we value and love them.

But when it comes to valuing **OURSELVES**,
it's an entirely different matter!

I'M TOO THIS,
TOO THAT
AND TOO MUCH
THE OTHER.

Be brave ... just for the sake of experiment ...
go to the mirror and say to your reflection

'I LOVE YOU'.

THAT'S A
BIG ASK!!

How did that **FEEL**?

Was it easy to do or did you feel a bit **FOOLISH**?

You might have actually found it
quite **CONFRONTING**.

Could you even **DO** it?

Try it once more. This time, notice
what feelings come up for you and especially notice
the **INTERNAL MESSAGES** that
run through your mind.

When self-love is missing, we tend to make unreasonable demands on **OTHERS** to fill the gap for us.

One way of seeing this is to imagine that if you were a house and you were pitching yourself to a prospective buyer, it might go something like this:

LOOK NO FURTHER! I'M PERFECT FOR YOU!

OF COURSE, I'LL NEED ALL OF YOUR ATTENTION OR I'LL FALL TO PIECES!

AND YOU'LL HAVE TO PROP ME UP BECAUSE MY FOUNDATIONS ARE SHAKY!

BUT YOU HAVE TO ADMIRE MY EXTERIOR!

15

We expect **OTHERS** to do for us that which we find almost impossible to do for **OURSELVES**. We expect unconditional love and acceptance from outside sources but have little more than **CONTEMPT** for ourselves.

In doing so, we ask others to agree to an extremely **LOPSIDED** relationship contract.

Hardly **FAIR**, is it?
Would you sign a contract like that?

There are three **POTENTIAL RELATIONSHIPS** with self and, thus, with others.

Maggie has so **LITTLE REGARD** for herself that she goes along with what she thinks other people want and **BURIES** her own needs and wants as a result.

> I LOSE, YOU WIN!

She takes on the responsibility for other people's **WELLBEING**, **CHOICES** and even their **MOODS**!

> I DON'T WANT TO MAKE A FUSS!

She does not set clear **BOUNDARIES** (and finds herself walked over!), cannot say **NO** and is **TERRIFIED** of offending.

17

Bruce needs you to bolster **HIM** up and he doesn't care if that saps **YOU** dry in the process.

> I WIN, YOU LOSE!

> CAN'T BE ME ... SO IT MUST BE YOU!

He is never **WRONG**, never **SORRY** and never **ACCOUNTABLE** for his own behaviour.

Bruce gets to love himself only at others' **EXPENSE**. He drains your energy and goodwill to boost his own **EGO**.

WE ALL WIN!

Jenny has found a **BALANCE** that means she does not have to **SACRIFICE** herself **OR** others in the process of being true to herself. She can **GIVE** and **TAKE** equally. She can **LOVE** and **BE LOVED**. Jenny has a healthy **LOVE OF SELF**.

This is what we will be aiming to achieve in this book.

WHY CAN'T WE

LOVE

OURSELVES?

'We are wont to condemn self-love; but what we
really mean to condemn is contrary to self-love.
It is that mixture of selfishness and self-hate
that permanently pursues us, that prevents us
from loving others and that prohibits us
from loving ourselves.'

Paul Valery

When we think of self-love, we often think of such a thing as being **SELF-INDULGENT, ARROGANT** or **DELUDED**.

BOY, DOESN'T *SHE* LOVE HERSELF?!!

This is because we often confuse self-love with **SELFISHNESS** or **SELF-ABSORPTION**, which, in its extreme form, is known as **NARCISSISM**.

THE STORY OF NARCISSUS

According to the Greek myth, Narcissus was an exceptionally **BEAUTIFUL** young man.

I'M UTTERLY GORG!

Unfortunately, he was also extremely **VAIN**.

Although he had many admirers, he rejected all of them in an **ARROGANT** and **CALLOUS** way.

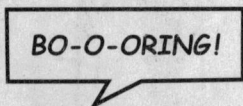

BO-O-ORING!

He even sent a rejected suitor a knife so he could **END IT ALL**!

WELL, *HELLO*!

One day, Narcissus came upon his own **REFLECTION** in a stream ...

... and fell in **LOVE** for the first time.

So **TRANSFIXED** was he by his own **BEAUTY**, he could not tear himself away ...

... until he eventually **STARVED** to **DEATH**.

WHAT IS THE DIFFERENCE BETWEEN SELF-LOVE AND NARCISSISM?

On the surface, the story of Narcissus seems to bear out our fears that to love the self means that we become **SELFISH** and develop an arrogant disregard for the needs and feelings of **OTHERS**.

But if we look at Narcissus a little more closely, we see that it isn't **HIMSELF** that he loves but his **REFLECTED** self.

He is actually incapable of love in any of its **PURE** forms, most of all, the **LOVE** of **SELF**.

In fact, it is a sense of feeling so miserably **INFERIOR** and **DEPENDENT** on others' approval that drives narcissistic behaviour in the first place.

Let's take a look at how this works:

Introducing our contemporary
NARCISSUS. We'll call him Tom.
(Apologies to all the **NICE**,
MODEST Toms out there!)

LUCKY YOU!

First of all, Tom has to hide
his True Self behind a **FACADE**,
or **FALSE SELF**.

(If Tom has self-love why
would he **NEED** the False
Self in the first place?)

This False Self is a hungry **MONSTER**.
It craves **CONSTANT ATTENTION** and
it will do anything to
get it, including using
FLATTERY, CHARM
and 'HELPFULNESS'.

ME
ME
ME
ME

WHO AM I AGAIN?

It has actually devoured Tom's True Self to the degree that Tom is no longer in touch with who he **REALLY IS**.

IT NEEDS A BIT OF WORK!

Tom relies on **REFLECTED** images of himself to feed his sense of self-worth.

ESSAY

SHE SAID IT WAS THE BEST THING SHE'D EVER READ!!

ESSAY

In order to see the best version of himself reflected back, he needs to **IMPRESS** others, so he invents **ACHIEVEMENTS**, **ABILITIES** and **ATTRIBUTES** which, in reality, seldom exist.

He has little or no real concern for others'
needs. He can only focus on getting his
OWN needs met.

> OK, SO I DIDN'T COME
> TO YOUR BIRTHDAY —
> BUT YOU'LL BE PLEASED
> TO KNOW I MET THIS
> HOT CHICK!

He lives only for the
**APPLAUSE, AFFIRMATION,
ADORATION** and **ATTENTION**
he needs others to supply.

> HEY, THAT'S *SILK*,
> YOU KNOW!

Because he has so little
SELF-AWARENESS,
he cannot feel **EMPATHY**,
SHARE others' **EMOTIONS**
or, of course, **LOVE** them.

WHAT DO I DO WITH THIS?

And because Tom is not **SELF-AWARE**, he could not possibly love his **TRUE SELF** and therefore has no idea **HOW** to love others.

I CAN'T LET ANYONE SEE THE REAL ME!

The irony is, Tom actually **WANTS** to love but he is so filled with **SELF-LOATHING**, he cannot engage with others in a truly loving way.

SIGH!

Just like Narcissus, he is ultimately condemned to **LONELINESS** because his need for others' approval is too great for others to meet. It is **INEXHAUSTIBLE**.

IMPORTANT NOTE

We've all met a genuine
narcissist, and most of us behave
in narcissistic ways at times
(especially when we feel insecure)!

In fact, there is a theory that we are
actually **ALWAYS** self-serving and that
we employ behaviours, even destructive
behaviours, that are driven by our **NEEDS**.
These may include the need to be **NOTICED**,
APPRECIATED, **NURTURED** or the
need to **PROTECT** ourselves.
(We'll explore this further later on.)

And there are times when it is actually **APPROPRIATE** or **NECESSARY** to be focussed on our own interests above those of others.

The key factor is that the **INTENTION** is not deliberately **HURTFUL**.

We've now explored narcissism, with its extremes of **SELF-INTEREST**, but what about the other end of the spectrum, where a person puts him- or herself **LAST** or even **HATES** him- or herself to the point of:

SELF-LOATHING?

IDIOT
DUD
FOOL

How many times a day do you **PUT YOURSELF DOWN?**

GOD I'M SO UGLY!!

How often do you **COMPARE** yourself unfavourably to others?

How often do you **REJECT COMPLIMENTS?**

How often do you **FIND FAULT** with yourself?

How often do you wish you were **OTHER** than **WHO YOU ARE?**

Basically, how do you **FEEL** about yourself?

I HATE MYSELF!

So, this leads to a crucial question:

Why would we come to **HATE** ourselves?

The origins of self-loathing

I

HATE

ME

'My great concern is not whether you have failed,
but whether you are content with your failure.'

Abraham Lincoln

In order to understand the
ORIGINS of low self-esteem,
it is important to take a
look back at **CHILDHOOD**.

CHILDHOOD is the time when
we are most **VULNERABLE**,
ACCEPTING and **DEEPLY INFLUENCED**
by those around us ...

... especially those
we rely on for
SUSTENANCE

SHELTER

and **SURVIVAL**.

As children, we tend to endow our guardians with almost **GOD-LIKE** power.

We do this because our very **SURVIVAL** relies on those in charge being ... well ... **IN CHARGE!**

These are our **PROTECTORS**, **NURTURERS** and **TEACHERS**.

We rely on them for **EVERYTHING**.

They teach us how **LIFE WORKS**, what **LOVE** is and how **POWERFUL** people interact with others.

LIFE'S HARD!

These early teachings and behavioural examples have considerable influence on the **BELIEFS** that we form about **LIFE**, **OTHERS** ...

... and **OURSELVES**, especially in terms of our **WORTH** and whether we deserve **LOVE** simply by being our **TRUE SELVES**.

BAD BOY!

In some cases, this may not be IDEAL.

Because the child needs its guardians to be PERFECT, it cannot afford to acknowledge any of their FLAWS ...

... so if the flaws are apparent, the child has no other option but to BLAME ITSELF!

I MADE HER SICK!

I MUST HAVE BEEN REALLY BAD!

HE'S ANGRY BECAUSE OF ME!

Of course, this is not always a case of 'BAD PARENTING'. We must remember that events may be coloured by a child's PERCEPTION and thus skewed in memory by the child's immature understanding at the time.

Let's take a look at how this might unfold:

Say that you are 'DADDY'S LITTLE PRINCESS'.

Every day when Daddy comes home from work, he scoops you into his arms and tells you he LOVES you.

Then, one day, Daddy
comes home from work
and he does not **SMILE**,
nor does he pick you up.

Instead, he
brushes past you,
GRIM-FACED,
barely patting you
on the head, strides into the bedroom and
SLAMS the door behind him.

You stand there,
STUNNED.

You aren't to
know that Daddy
has just **LOST
HIS JOB**.

You only know that he didn't greet you in the same way.

This could only mean **ONE THING**.

DADDY DOESN'T LOVE ME ANY MORE!

I MUST BE BAD!!

And there can only be one reason for **THAT**!

So, from this example, we can see how even in a fairly **INNOCENT** exchange, a child may begin to form a set of **BELIEFS** that suggest that her worth and capacity to be loved are conditional upon her being **PERFECT**.

Circumstances in a more **UNSTABLE** or **STRICT** environment may lead to a child having to '**DISOWN**' whole aspects of self to be **ACCEPTED** or **APPRECIATED** ...

I CAN'T BE ME AND BE *LOVED*!

IT'S MY FAULT THIS IS HAPPENING! I MUST DO BETTER!

... or, in the worst-case scenario, to avoid **PUNISHMENT** or **TRAUMA**.

As a result, a set of **DAMAGING BELIEFS** may emerge:

I'M NOT GOOD ENOUGH

I DON'T BELONG

I'M STUPID

I'M UNLOVABLE

It is these **BELIEFS** that form the basis of the **EMOTIONAL PROGRAMMING** which causes us to **REACT** to situations in a certain way.

We forget that a situation itself is **NEUTRAL**! It is **WE** who place **MEANING** on events.

It is our **PERCEPTION** of things, based on past experiences, which causes us to see things as **GOOD** or **BAD**, **SAFE** or **DANGEROUS**, **COMFORTING** or **UNSETTLING**.

Imagine that in your mind there is a **FILING CABINET** where all your experiences are stored.

When there is a strong **EMOTIONAL CHARGE** on an experience, the file is labelled accordingly and stored away.

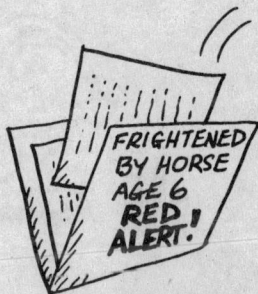

That file will remain dormant until a similar set of circumstances opens it up again and the same **EMOTIONS** resurface.

WE'RE GOING RIDING!

Everyone has a different set of **FILES**. This means we each have a different **RESPONSE** to the things that happen to us.

I LOVE RAINY DAYS!

RAINY DAYS DEPRESS ME!

The beliefs about our **WORTH** formed during childhood have a powerful impact on self-esteem and, as a result, we make **CHOICES** based on what we believe we **DESERVE**.

And we make life choices which both come from and **REINFORCE** these beliefs.

These **BELIEFS** become the only **REALITY** that we experience.

LIFE SUX!

DING DONG!

THINGS NEVER WORK OUT FOR ME!

We tend to see only what we **EXPECT** to see.

There may be limitless **POSSIBILITIES** but if we believe that we have few **CHOICES**, that is what will be apparent to us.

THERE'S NOTHING THERE!

If the choices you make undermine your self-worth, you end up in a **VICIOUS CIRCLE**.

I'M A LOSER!

I'LL FAIL!

F

NO-ONE WILL EVER LOVE ME!

And your self-worth plummets even **FURTHER**.

Whatever you focus on will tend to **MANIFEST**, simply because you filter out anything that doesn't fit your expectations.

WHY AM I SO LONELY?

HEY, YOU ASKED FOR IT!

47

In particular, if you **DISOWN** yourself, you will call to you experiences that bear out that belief and make it seem **TRUE**.

Our biggest fears are **ABANDONMENT** and **REJECTION**, and these are the driving force behind all our defensive and self-protecting behaviours including, amazingly, **SELF-LOATHING**.

If you have not been able to express your **ANGER** and **HURT** outwardly, you will turn it on **YOURSELF**.

THEY WERE SO MEAN TO ME!

I'LL BE SO MISERABLE THEY'LL SEE WHAT THEY'VE DONE!

The childlike need to **BELONG**, coupled with the fear of **REJECTION**, may result in your spending your life either ...

CAN'T CONTROL ME!

IF I KEEP EVERYONE HAPPY, THEY'LL LIKE ME!

... **REBELLING** or **ACCOMMODATING**.
(Or a bit of BOTH!)

Of course, this tends to do even more
DAMAGE. The thing that once **PROTECTED**
you is now the thing that **WOUNDS** you.

SCARED
LONELY
CUT OFF
HURT

However, dropping
your **DEFENCES** means
that you now risk
revealing your **TRUE
SELF** and, thus, your
VULNERABILITY.

Your **FEARS** and **DOUBTS**
become exposed.

Looking at this may feel **CHALLENGING**, but how can you **CHANGE** that which you don't **ACKNOWLEDGE**?

Things are always **SCARIER** in the **DARK**. Turn on a **LIGHT** and you see them as the **ILLUSIONS** (or rather, **DELUSIONS**) that they really are.

Becoming whole means reclaiming
and making peace with your
AUTHENTIC SELF.

We will work through this.

The fear of change

IT'S ALL ABOUT ME

'You must be the change you wish to see
in the world.'

Mahatma Gandhi

It is one thing to establish the **CAUSES** of low self-esteem and another to **UNHOOK** from them.

Consider this statement:

> # I am not
> # what happened to me —
> # I am what
> # I chose to become.

Some people may carry very deep wounds from their past, which lead to the mistaken idea that they are **WRONG**, **BAD** or **UNWORTHY** and, worse still, that they **DESERVE TO BE PUNISHED**.

I DESERVE TO SUFFER!

We now reach a point where it is necessary to apply some **TOUGH SELF-LOVE** if you wish to **MOVE ON**.

We come to the **KEY QUESTION**:

DO YOU **REALLY** WANT TO MOVE ON?

You may think that the obvious answer is 'Yes' but this is not always straightforward.

FRANKLY, I FIND HAPPINESS **BORING!**

Indeed, **SUFFERING** can be very **ADDICTIVE!**

There can be several blocks to **MOVING ON** and these come in the form of **EMOTIONAL PAYOFFS**.

It has been said that **EVERY HUMAN BEHAVIOUR** has an **EMOTIONAL PAYOFF**.

Essentially what this means is that we only do that which feels **'GOOD'** and offers **'REWARDS'** or, perhaps more accurately, we choose behaviours which cause the least **PAIN**.

We only let go of such behaviours when they cease to create 'payoffs' or when we become **AWARE** that we're seeking such payoffs and understand that the behaviours create more problems than the payoffs can solve.

> WHAT POSSIBLE **BENEFIT** CAN THERE BE FROM FEELING **BAD** ALL THE TIME?

> I FIND IT ALMOST **INSULTING** TO SUGGEST THAT I AM THIS WAY TO 'GET' SOMETHING! I AM GENUINELY **SUFFERING!**

Much of this is about basic **SURVIVAL** and mostly **UNCONSCIOUS**. These devices are actually constructed to help us cope or to keep us 'safe' from even **GREATER** perceived 'dangers'.

Let's take a look:

BONDING WITH OTHERS

Sharing our displeasure, suffering or unhappiness provides a strange form of **INTIMACY**, even with virtual strangers. If your suffering equals my suffering, **BINGO**! We can be friends for life!

In this case, the **PAYOFF** may be **BONDING** but the **PRICE** is that it is necessary to hold on to the **STRUGGLE**.

If you want to test how this works, try this:

DON'T WHINGE TO ANYONE ABOUT ANYTHING FOR A WEEK!

YIKES!

(If you manage a week, why not try it **PERMANENTLY?!**)

GETTING ATTENTION

I'M WORRIED ABOUT YOU!

If you have difficulty getting the **NURTURE**, **SUPPORT** or **LOVE** you need from others in an authentic way, you may find that you receive much more attention when you are in **CRISIS**.

Even **NEGATIVE** attention can feel better than **NO** attention!

OH, GET OVER IT!

SHE ONLY PICKS ON ME!

INVERTED PRIDE

I'M SO MESSED UP THERE'S NO HOPE FOR ME!

Strange as it may seem, it can be almost a source of pride to win the **MOST UNHAPPY, MOST ANXIOUS** or **MOST TROUBLED** award.

The first **PAYOFF** is that you feel special. The second **PAYOFF** is that, since there's no hope for you, you don't even have to **TRY**.

The **PRICE** is that all you have left is your **TITLE**.

PROTECTION

> NO-ONE'S GOING TO GET CLOSE TO ME!

If you have been very hurt in the past, self-loathing can be an effective **ARMOUR** against allowing anyone the chance of possibly hurting you again. The **PAYOFF** may be that you feel '**SAFE**'. The **PRICE** is that you are **LONELY**.

FEAR OF CHANGE

> BUT WILL I STILL BE LOVED IF I'M DIFFERENT?

Becoming whole may mean making changes that are more threatening than staying **STUCK**.

Making changes may lead to some **TOUGH DECISIONS**, such as:

NOT ON!

LEAVING AN or **ASSERTING** or **BEING MORE**
UNHEALTHY   **YOURSELF**   **INDEPENDENT**
RELATIONSHIP

... all of which may feel daunting.

The **PAYOFF** for **NOT** changing is that you don't have to **FACE** these challenges.

The **PRICE** is that there's little chance of things **IMPROVING**.

The way forward from this mindset is to recognise that the one thing that can never be taken away from you is **CHOICE**.

Of course, for every **CHOICE** there are **CONSEQUENCES**.

The following are all **CHOICES**:

TO KEEP RELIVING
THE PAST

I CAN'T HELP
WHAT HAPPENS
TO ME!

TO SEE YOURSELF
AS A VICTIM

IT'S THEIR
FAULT I'M
UNHAPPY!

TO BLAME OTHERS
FOR WHERE YOU
FIND YOURSELF

IT'LL NEVER
WORK OUT!

TO EXPECT THE
WORSE

MEA
CULPA!

TO BEAT YOURSELF
UP OVER MISTAKES

BAD   WRONG
   UGLY
AWFUL   TERRIBLE

TO THINK
NEGATIVELY

AND TO STAY
STUCK.

Even if you were constantly **CRITICISED**, **PUT DOWN**, **TEASED** or **ABUSED** it is now your **CHOICE** whether you continue to **BELIEVE** or **INVEST** in this construction.

HEY, I'M NOT THAT!

If someone led you to believe that you were unlovable, has it ever occurred to you that you can actually **DISAGREE**?

STOP PROVING THEM RIGHT!

IMPORTANT NOTE

If you think you deserve
to **SUFFER**, no-one is going to
change your mind
about that, except **YOU**!

Embracing the lost self

ME AND MY SHADOW

'Don't find fault. Find a remedy.'

Henry Ford

Everyone has a **SHADOW** side.

This is the part (or parts) of ourselves that we try to **DISOWN**, because we see it (or we were taught to see it) as **UNACCEPTABLE** or **UNLOVABLE**.

Especially in societies that value 'manners' or 'refinement', we are often taught to repress this 'unpleasantness' and show only the best or '**NICEST**' aspects of ourselves in order to be **ACCEPTED**.

This means we're constantly in a **LOPSIDED** state, trying to keep **EVERYBODY** happy!

However, unless the **SHADOW** is acknowledged and embraced, it has a tendency to loom even **LARGER**.

The more you **REPRESS** the shadow side, the more likely it is to **SHOW UP**!

WHEN MILDRED TAKES OVER SHE THINKS SHE'S A GOODY GOODY.

BUT SHE'S REALLY A CONTROL FREAK!

It is easy to observe your own **SHADOW** side in action by noticing how easily you become **ANNOYED** with aspects of others.

The behaviours that bother you most '**OUT THERE**' are usually a reflection of those you have disowned in **YOURSELF**!

JOE ALWAYS FEELS SORRY FOR HIMSELF! IT'S NOT LIKE HE HAS PROBLEMS LIKE MINE!

The next time
you find yourself
criticising another,
ASK YOURSELF:

WHEN DO I
DO THE SAME
THING?

If you wish to have a more loving relationship
with yourself, it is important that you
RECLAIM those '**UNDESIRABLE**' aspects
of your personality by making them more
ACCEPTABLE to yourself.

One way to do this is to see the **SHADOW**
side (of yourself and others) as being not so
much **BAD** as **CONTRASTING**.

In some Eastern countries,
there are decorations
on buildings which look
something like **THIS**:

On one side, a face is looking towards the
'happier' or more 'positive' aspects of life.
The face on the other side looks towards the
'darker' or more 'negative' aspects of life.

The face in the middle represents adopting a position that embraces **BOTH** aspects of life (or self) as being a necessary balance of **OPPOSITES** to make the **WHOLE**.

The thought behind this is that you can't **APPRECIATE** or even **EXPERIENCE** something if you have not experienced what it **ISN'T**.

So, you can't really know:

DAY	JOY	PEACE

WITHOUT	**WITHOUT**	**WITHOUT**

NIGHT	SORROW	UNREST

Refer to any basic book on astrology and you will see that every sign has its **STRENGTHS** and **WEAKNESSES**.

Let's take a look:

ARIES

Dynamic	Aggressive
Honest	Argumentative
Energetic	Rebellious

TAURUS

Steadfast	Stodgy
Controlled	Stubborn
Tasteful	Self-indulgent

GEMINI

Expressive	Chatterbox
Energetic	Chaotic
Innovative	Undisciplined

CANCER

Patient	Procrastinating
Accommodating	Long-suffering
Sensitive	Moody

LEO

Powerful	Bossy
Self-confident	Arrogant
Sturdy	Combative

VIRGO

Refined	Fussy
Methodical	Unyielding
Virtuous	Puritanical

LIBRA

Charming	Pretentious
Balanced	Indecisive
Peacemaker	Complacent

SCORPIO

Passionate	Intense
Courageous	Volatile
Thorough	Obsessed

SAGITTARIUS

Cheerful	Unrealistic
Honest	Blunt
Vibrant	Frazzled

CAPRICORN

Self-disciplined	Stern
Responsible	Workaholic
Self-assured	Aloof

AQUARIUS

Original	Flaky
Spontaneous	Impulsive
Spirited	Unreliable

PISCES

Giving	Needy
Devoted	Complacent
Intuitive	Dreamer

As you can see from the listed character traits, **NO-ONE** gets off with **FREE PASS**!

However, you don't need to believe in astrology to observe that **EVERYONE**, without exception, has their 'good' points and 'not so good' points.

These same strengths and weaknesses, such as those listed in the given examples, are **TWO SIDES** of the **SAME COIN** and will be deemed to be '**DESIRABLE**' or '**UNDESIRABLE**' depending on several factors:

How these traits are **USED**

I'M A NATURAL LEADER!

PUT THAT THERE!

BOSSY!

How these traits are **PERCEIVED** by others

And whether the person displaying these traits is **COMFORTABLE** with him– or herself.

What would happen if you took away the 'not so great' side of someone's character?

Well, let's see:

Here's **GEORGE**. He's a manager of a large firm and has to make some **TOUGH DECISIONS**.

I'M SORRY, BUT I'M GOING TO HAVE TO LET YOU GO.

THEY ALL HATE ME!

One day George decides that he'd rather be **POPULAR**, which means keeping everybody **HAPPY**!

In his attempts to do this, George **BENDS OVER BACKWARDS**.

Everyone is **PLEASED**, all right!

Well, everyone except **GEORGE**, that is!

Many of us do the same as George. We bury whole aspects of ourselves to be 'nice', then feel hurt and blame others when this is abused.

WE TEACH OTHERS HOW TO TREAT US

There is a saying attributed to St Augustine:

'IF EVERYONE APPROVES OF WHAT YOU'RE DOING, I STRONGLY URGE YOU TO CHANGE WHAT YOU'RE DOING!'

Our greatest fear is **REJECTION** but in fearing this, we end up **REJECTING** aspects of ourselves.

When you befriend yourself, when you are truly your own **SUPPORT** team, **CHEER SQUAD** and **ADMIRER**, the fear of rejection from others diminishes.

WARTS 'N' ALL, EH?

WELL, GREEN IS MY COLOUR!

This means making **PEACE** with and **ACCEPTING ALL** aspects of yourself, because, let's face it, they're what make you, **YOU**!

If you are **PROUD** of who you are and what you do, then what is there to **HIDE**?

If you feel no **SHAME** about being the way you are, if you **ACCEPT** yourself in all your colours, then what is there left for others to reject?

And even if they do, **SO WHAT? BIG DEAL! THEIR LOSS**!

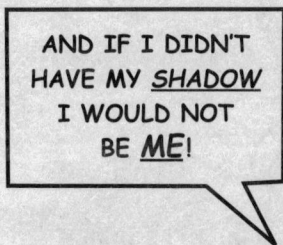

TAKE IT OR LEAVE IT, THAT'S THE PACKAGE!

AND IF I DIDN'T HAVE MY <u>SHADOW</u> I WOULD NOT BE <u>ME</u>!

Forgiveness and self-love

I
FORGIVE
ME

'Forgiveness is the fragrance the violet
sheds on the heel that has crushed it.'

Mark Twain

Of course, there may be some things that you do or have done that you're **NOT** proud of!

But how can you truly **LOVE** yourself if you can't or haven't **FORGIVEN** yourself?

A LACK OF FORGIVENESS OF SELF CAN RESULT IN:

INDIFFERENCE towards, **NEGLECT** of or even **CONTEMPT** for your own needs

THAT'S ALL I DESERVE.

SELF-DESTRUCTIVE

behaviours and attitudes

Being unable to receive **LOVE** or **CARING** from others

and
Feeling
SELF-PITY.

Do you **REALLY** deserve to **SUFFER?**

A chronic addiction to **GUILT** does nothing to **REMEDY** a situation or change the circumstances.

Instead, it keeps you trapped in a prison of **SELF-LOATHING** and self-imposed **MARTYRDOM**, which doesn't do anything to solve the problems you've caused.

If you don't **LOVE** or even **LIKE** yourself chances are that **GUILT** is the thing that is blocking you.

I JUST DON'T FIT IN WITH MOST PEOPLE.

So what do you feel **GUILTY** about?

Is it **YOUR** fault if others don't **GET** you? Do they really **HAVE** to? What if you were **PROUD** of your uniqueness?

BUT I'VE BEEN REJECTED SO OFTEN!

Most people have only a small number of **REAL** friends. Others might **SEEM** to be more popular **BUT** this is just a surface impression. The important question is: do you **REJECT** yourself?

MY LIFE JUST DOESN'T WORK!

Compared to **WHOSE?** Do you have some **IDEALISED** notion of a **PERFECT** life? (Perhaps from television?) Your life is **PERFECT** in the sense that you are exactly positioned to figure out what you're here to figure out. Any **CHALLENGES** are part of that process. Would you be **MOTIVATED** to **CHANGE** and **GROW** otherwise?

BUT WHENEVER I GIVE LOVE I GET HURT!

The **KEY WORD** here is 'GIVE'. You either **GIVE** or you don't. If you're **GIVING** to **GET**, the 'gift' has become a **BRIBE**.

If you **GIVE** your love freely, is it your fault (or even your **PROBLEM**) if the recipient doesn't **RESPECT** that gift?

If you have low self-esteem, you can pretty much blame **YOURSELF** for **EVERYTHING** ...

MY FAULT!

... which is actually rather **SELF-CENTRED**, when you really think about it!

ALL RIGHT ... I'M READY TO MOVE ON. HOW DO YOU SUGGEST I DO THIS?

FORGIVING YOURSELF INVOLVES:

Accepting that you are a **HUMAN BEING** ...

I'M NOT SUPERMAN!

OK, SO I LOST MY TEMPER!

... who makes **MISTAKES** just like every other **HUMAN BEING** ...

I GET A BIT AGGRO WHEN I DRINK. BETTER WATCH IT!

... and if you are willing to **LEARN** from your **MISTAKES** ...

... instead of being **STUCK** in **REGRET** ...

I WISH I HADN'T SAID THAT! I'M A BAD FRIEND!

I THINK I'LL PASS, THANKS!

... you can do **BETTER** next time!

FORGIVENESS is something of a **CURE-ALL** as it lowers **BLOOD PRESSURE**, improves **GENERAL HEALTH** and improves your chances **OF LONGEVITY!**

TAKE ONE OF THESE DAILY FOR THE REST OF YOUR LIFE!

4 GIVE

Studies have shown that highly self-forgiving women are **THREE** times less likely to develop clinical depression than those who are prone to self-blame. For men, it's **SEVEN** times less likely!

Learn to recognise the difference between a **HEALTHY CONSCIENCE** and **TOXIC SHAME**.

A great way to feel good about yourself is simply knowing that you're motivated by kindness.

CHECK IN regularly with yourself about the '**OKAYNESS**' of what you do or say.

BUT HOW DO I KNOW THAT I'M NOT JUST TRYING TO KEEP EVERYBODY (AND NOT MYSELF) HAPPY AS I DID BEFORE?

INTENTION
IS EVERYTHING!

A good way to gauge this is to ask yourself whether you are coming from a **LOVING** position, not just for others, but for yourself, also. If you're coming from **THE RIGHT INTENTION** you can be **HONEST** and know you are not being **HURTFUL**, **INSINCERE** or **MANIPULATIVE**.

Use **GUILT** as a **BAROMETER**.
Don't make it a **PRISON**!

The important question is: Who is setting the **RULES** on how **YOUR** life should be? Who is your **CONSCIENCE**?

And if **YOU'RE** not, why is that?

BE WHO YOU ARE ...

JUST DO THE RIGHT THING BY YOURSELF AND OTHERS.

And what is **THE RIGHT THING?**

St Augustine again ...

LOVE ...
AND DO WHAT
YOU LIKE!

Forgiving others

I

FORGIVE

YOU

'To forgive is to set a prisoner free and discover
that the prisoner was you.'

Lewis B. Smedes

OK, I FEEL AS THOUGH I'VE FORGIVEN MYSELF BUT THERE ARE SOME PEOPLE IN MY LIFE WHO I CAN NEVER FORGIVE!

If you want to get to **SELF-LOVE**, you will need to forgive others, too.

WHY SHOULD I?

Because holding onto **HURT** or **RESENTMENT** is actually **MORE HARMFUL** to **YOU** than the person who has hurt you!

HUH? THEY HURT ME VERY BADLY! THEY'VE RUINED MY LIFE!

OK ... here's a **QUESTION:**

What is this thing we call **THE PAST?**

> UMM, THINGS THAT
> HAPPENED TO ME!

And how do you **KNOW** that these
things **HAPPENED?**

> WELL, BECAUSE I
> REMEMBER THEM,
> OF COURSE!

OK, so let's **SIDESTEP** a little for a moment.

> CAN'T WAIT
> TO SEE WHERE
> THIS IS GOING!

Imagine a **ROOM FULL** of people ...

... do you think they would **ALL** feel equally **COMFORTABLE**?

Some would feel **JUST RIGHT** ...

... some too **COLD** ...

... and some **TOO HOT**!

So, which of those people is **RIGHT**?

NONE OF THEM ...
OR MAYBE ALL OF THEM ...
I DON'T KNOW!

YEAH ... SO?

So, would it be fair to say from this example that everyone in that room has a different **OPINION** on what is happening?

Well, **MEMORIES** work this way, too.

They have **IMPACT**, depending on how much **MEANING** we place on them and, more importantly, how **MUCH** we keep focussing on that **MEANING** and for how **LONG**!

SO, CHANGE THE MEANING AND YOU CHANGE THE PAST?

EXACTLY!

SO, I GUESS YOU'RE GOING TO TELL ME THAT ONE WAY TO CHANGE THE MEANING IS TO FORGIVE!

BINGO!

BUT HOW DO I DO THAT? WHAT I WENT THROUGH WAS TERRIBLE!

Indeed it was, but even though someone else **HURT** you (or you caused yourself or others **HARM**) it is the ongoing **TORTURE** that you inflict on yourself as a result that does even more **DAMAGE**!

FORGIVENESS means making a decision to no longer **PUNISH YOURSELF** for that which you or another did to you.

It means:

Wholeheartedly **RE-ENTERING** life
instead of staying **STUCK** in the event

Being free of the burden of **ANGER** at
someone that **YOU'RE** carrying!

Claiming **RESPONSIBILITY** for your own
life and leaving others to **THEIRS**

I CAN ONLY LIVE
ONE PERSON'S LIFE
AT A TIME ...
MINE!

I'M *STILL* WAITING FOR THEM TO SAY SORRY FOR WHAT HAPPENED 20 YEARS AGO!

and

Developing **MASTERY** over your own wounds instead of hoping your 'enemy' will somehow heal them for you.

Changing the meaning of past events into the positive will occur if you **RISE ABOVE** them.

If you create a **GOOD** situation out of a **BAD** one, then the **MEANING** of the event has changed.

Many notable humanitarians have used their difficult past experiences as a motivator to help others who have suffered in a similar way.

And many of these people had to do some **SERIOUS FORGIVING** in order to move on!

OK, let's be **HONEST**. There are some people who do some really, really awful things in the world and that may take a fair bit of **FORGIVING** on your part.

But to really love yourself, you need to set yourself **FREE** of the things that hold you back from realising your true brilliance.

It may be **HELPFUL** to see **FORGIVENESS** of others as a good old **DETOX**!

RIGHT, TIME I OFFLOADED ALL THIS DEAD WEIGHT!

THE PAST

Recognise that staying **ANGRY** with someone **HOLDS YOU TO THEM!**

IMPORTANT NOTE

Many people mistake **FORGIVENESS** with **CONDONING** a bad act but, rather, it is **UNHOOKING** from the **POWER** that **PAST EVENTS** have over your **HAPPINESS** in the **PRESENT**.

Say Larry bingles your brand-new car.

You could stay **ANGRY** with Larry long after the event ...

... in which case, you will no longer **ENJOY** having your car ...

... because your **ANGER** hits you every time you sit behind the wheel.

This won't happen if you **FORGIVE** him ...

OK. I FORGIVE YOU.

PHEW! THANKS! I'LL MAKE IT UP TO YOU.

... because you're now free to **ENJOY** your car (and Larry) again!

FORGIVENESS says, 'I can't change the **PAST**. It's **OVER**, it's **DONE**. It's what happens **NEXT** that is important.'

And what you make of events is what you are willing to **LEARN** about **YOURSELF** from them.

WELL, I GUESS I KNEW LARRY WAS A BAD DRIVER BUT I LET HIM TALK ME INTO IT!

So, what have you **LEARNED** about yourself from this?

THAT I NEED TO STAND MY GROUND!

So if Larry has taught you something **IMPORTANT**, in the end, what does he need to be **FORGIVEN** for?

OH I GET IT — IT WASN'T HIS FAULT I DIDN'T SAY NO! HMM ...

BUT HE DOESN'T GET TO DRIVE MY CAR AGAIN!

The **PAST** can be an ongoing (and even worse) **MESS** or it can be **TRANSFORMED** into a motivating factor to do **BETTER** or be a **BETTER PERSON**. You can always be **BIGGER** than someone who is **SMALL** enough to hurt others!

AND TO THINK I LET HIM HAVE POWER OVER MY WHOLE WELLBEING!

That's how you become a **WINNER**!

And remember: **FORGIVENESS** is a **TWO-WAY** street. Often we want to be **FORGIVEN** but do not want to **FORGIVE**.

We want others to take into account the **CIRCUMSTANCES** that led us to behave in a less-than-ideal way.

> I WAS UNDER STRESS! IT JUST CAME OUT WRONG! I DIDN'T MEAN TO HURT YOU!

We hope that others will see past the **BEHAVIOUR** and understand the inner **PAIN** or **UNREST** that caused us to **LOSE OURSELVES**, or that we had our own **REASONS** for doing what we did.

And we hope that they will still see the **GOOD** in us beneath the act.

Are you **BIG** enough to return the **FAVOUR**?

LOVING ME, LOVING YOU

'If you aren't good at loving yourself, you will have a difficult time loving anyone, since you'll resent the time and energy you give another person that you aren't even giving to yourself.'

Barbara de Angelis

If you don't have a strong sense of self-worth, you will tend to be overly reliant on the **APPROVAL** of others.

At the same time, you will most likely be **SENSITIVE** to signs of **REJECTION** if you believe that your worth rests on what others think of you.

Unfortunately, others can be **UNRELIABLE** in supplying what you need when you need it because they too are usually seeking the **SAME** reassurance as **YOU** are!

Dealing with others can be **CHALLENGING**, however it is through our interactions with others that we have the greatest opportunity to learn about **OURSELVES**.

OTHERS ARE OUR MIRRORS

The bottom line is that what **SOMEONE ELSE** does is not the issue; it is what **YOU** do in response that is the key factor.

You can't **CHANGE** someone else.

IF ONLY HE'D CHANGE, THEN I COULD LOVE HIM UNCONDITIONALLY!

Not only is this beyond your **POWER** (unless the person already wants to change), it's not your **JOB** to do so, nor is it your **RIGHT**.

The only one you can change is YOU.

It may be helpful to notice, in your exchanges
with others, when you

GAIN POWER,
LOSE POWER or
GIVE YOUR POWER AWAY.

You give your power away when you:

Make others into
**AUTHORITY
FIGURES** or
EXPERTS on
your life

> TELL ME
> WHAT TO DO!

Share too many **INTIMATE DETAILS**
with others before **TRUST** is established

> ... AND THEN I HAD
> THIS OPERATION
> AND THEN ...

Think that you **HAVE TO, GOT TO, SHOULD, MUST** or that you are **FORCED** to do anything you don't choose to

or
Feel the need
to **EXPLAIN** or
JUSTIFY YOURSELF.

ASK YOURSELF:

Do I **TRUST** myself?

Do I really know
what **I WANT?**

Do I know what's **BEST** for me?

DO I LIKE THAT?

If you don't trust yourself, know what you want or what's best for you, how can others give you what you **NEED**?

The people you attract into your life are your greatest **TEACHERS** — especially the ones who **BUG** you the most.

If you find that people are **BEHAVING BADLY** towards you, ask yourself:

What is their behaviour telling **ME** about **MYSELF**?

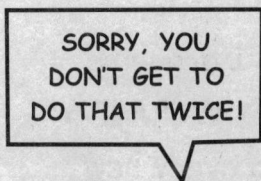

KICK ME

SORRY, YOU DON'T GET TO DO THAT TWICE!

What might you do **DIFFERENTLY** in the future to ensure a better outcome?

Do I set clear **BOUNDARIES**?

Do I silently **CONDONE** bad behaviour?

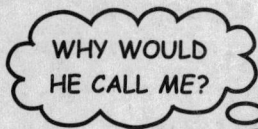

HE DOESN'T RESPECT ME — BUT I'LL STAY!

WHY WOULD HE CALL ME?

Am I **EXPECTING** disappointment or rejection?

Am I dragging **OLD WOUNDS** into every new situation?

SHE'LL HURT ME TOO!

Do I expect everyone's **RULE BOOK** to be the same as mine?

LIFE MY WAY

What **MESSAGES** about myself am I putting out there that others may be responding to?

YIKES!

IF YOU WANT TO BE LOVED
YOU NEED TO BE LOVABLE
and
YOU NEED TO BELIEVE
THAT YOU ARE
which means
LOVING YOURSELF
because
LOVE ATTRACTS LOVE.

Even the Bible says 'Love thy neighbour **AS** thyself' — not '**INSTEAD OF**'!

How would you complete this statement?

'I GIVE LOVE AND I GET ...'

RIPPED OFF
LIED TO
ABANDONED
HURT
USED

If the answer is not **'LOVED IN RETURN'** use this to **INFORM** yourself about the changes you may need to make.

This might mean:

Saying **NO**

NOT AGAIN!

DEAR JOHN

Being **CLEAR**

WE NEED TO TALK!

Being HONEST

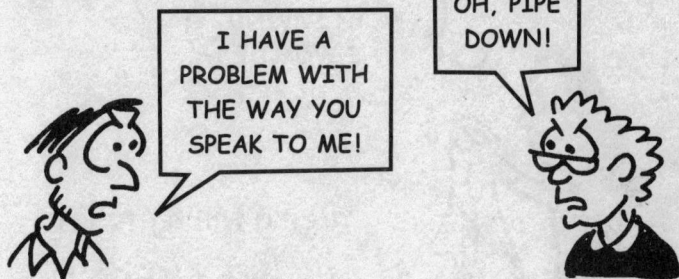

Risking UNPOPULARITY

Leaving others to make their own MISTAKES and find their own SOLUTIONS

I'M THROUGH WITH SAVING THE WORLD!

or

Being willing to let things be **MESSY**.

If you find yourself **CHAFING** against others, see if you are able to identify a **REPEATING THEME** behind the problem.

ASK YOURSELF:

WHAT CAN I LEARN FROM THIS?

Use the experience to **PUSH YOURSELF FORWARD**.

Old patterns will tend to **REPEAT** only because they have not yet been **RESOLVED**.

THAT AGAIN?!

If you are willing to **IDENTIFY** and **ADDRESS** your own **BLOCKS** and **HEAL** your own **INSECURITIES** as they come up in encounters with others, you will be more likely to see others as **TEACHERS** than as **THREATS**.

And if you don't **AGREE** with the way someone behaves you no longer need to take it **ON BOARD**.

Ironically, one of the best ways to **FIND** yourself is to **LOSE** yourself!

When your focus is constantly **INWARD**, you will have a tendency to **OVERTHINK**, **OVERANALYSE** and **OVERWHELM** yourself.

When you are locked into **YOURSELF**, you can become overly **SELF-CONSCIOUS**.

One of the **BEST** ways to **LOSE** yourself is through **GIVING** to others.

However, it's important that you make the distinction between **GIVING** of yourself and **DEPLETING** yourself.

Again, let's reflect on the notion of **GIVING**.

A true gift doesn't have a **PRICE TAG**.

If you give with the expectation of something in **RETURN**, you set yourself up for possible **DISAPPOINTMENT** or **RESENTMENT**.

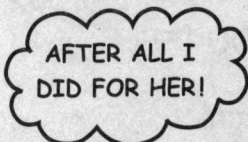

AFTER ALL I DID FOR HER!

And if you find yourself **DEPLETED** by all your 'GIVING', you may need to identify your true motives.

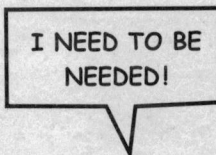

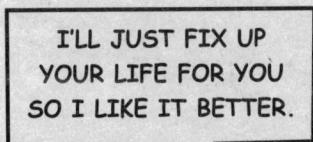

I NEED TO BE NEEDED!

I'LL JUST FIX UP YOUR LIFE FOR YOU SO I LIKE IT BETTER.

It's one thing to be **HELPFUL** and another to find yourself feeling **EMPTY**, **STRESSED** and **EXHAUSTED** as a result.

That's not doing **ANYONE**, least of all **YOURSELF**, any favours!

Think of it this way:

If you jumped into a raging sea to **RESCUE** people ...

... and you didn't wear your **LIFE JACKET** ...

... how many people would you **SAVE**?

You will always be of more help to another if you yourself are **SHIPSHAPE**!

And helping others can be an effective tool for 'PERFECTING YOURSELF' because:

It **REFLECTS** back to you the **BEST** of yourself

You **MATTER** to someone and

Your own circumstances are put in **PERSPECTIVE**.

True giving lifts both the **GIVER** and the **RECEIVER** and through **GIVING** without any **ATTACHMENT** or **AGENDA** you learn to:

LOVE UNCONDITIONALLY.

Which means:
ACCEPTING others
AS THEY ARE

Embracing
DIFFERENCES

and
Seeing that **WE'RE ALL
IN THIS TOGETHER**,
doing the **BEST** we can.

And from this viewpoint, you can come to
see that you really are a **GOOD PERSON**
and that you're a **VALUED** member of the
HUMAN RACE.

A self-actualised person is **ATTRACTIVE**
because they:

DEMAND less

WHY DIDN'T
YOU CALL?

WE SPOKE
15 MINUTES
AGO!

CONTROL less

FRET less

BLAME less

and

Aim for **WIN/WIN** relationships.

If you stand by **YOU**, someone else is also likely to.

Standing by yourself in tough times

LOVE

THE ONE
YOU'RE WITH

'I saw the angel in the marble and carved
until I set him free.'

Michelangelo

Surely the most important time to stand by **YOURSELF** is when it feels as though others have turned their backs on you.

Yet this is often the time when we tend to beat ourselves up the most, either by feeling **ANGER** towards others (and we've seen the damage that can do in the chapter on forgiveness!) or by taking on the entire **BLAME** ourselves and being consumed by **GUILT** and **SELF-LOATHING**.

Though it may seem difficult to maintain a healthy self-image when all that is being reflected back to you is your apparent shortcomings, it is vitally important at these times that you step in and **BE THERE FOR YOU.**

DOING SO MEANS THAT YOU:

Gain a **HEALTHIER PERSPECTIVE** on the situation instead of falling into a complete heap

Take things 'on the chin' instead of **SHUTTING DOWN**

Move out of a negative emotional zone more **QUICKLY**

Build greater **RESILIENCE**
and **PRIDE** in yourself
and gain **CONFIDENCE**
by seeing through the
tough stuff

PAT
PAT

Be more likely to
attract similarly
self-loving
(and therefore
'**NUTRITIOUS**')
people

and
Be more likely to resolve issues with others
with greater **CALM** and **OBJECTIVITY**.

OK, THIS IS HOW
IT IS FOR ME ...

I'M LISTENING.

The first step is learning to 'STAY OUT' emotionally in a crisis.

What this means is that when we have low self-esteem, we usually respond to what we perceive as criticism or rejection by immediately closing down into 'HURT MODE'.

When we feel DISEMPOWERED, INSECURE or THREATENED, we tend to turn to one of the following PROTECTIVE devices:

RUN AWAY

BECOME ANGRY
AND DEFENSIVE

HIT BACK

SULK

SHUT DOWN

BECOME 'HELPLESS'

BLAME THE OTHER or **OURSELVES**

APOLOGISE TOO READILY or

AGREE, THEN DO SOMETHING UNDERHANDED
(passive aggression).

These are all forms of childlike '**COLLAPSE**'. Every time you collapse in this way, you undermine your own power and you end up feeling **WORSE** about yourself.

'Staying out' means catching yourself when you are about to close down into hurt by recognising that this is the **CHILD** in you and calling on your **ADULT** self to step in.

> BUT I'M NOT A CHILD! I'M 36 YEARS OLD! I'M *MATURE!*

Yes, but how **OLD** do you feel when you're **UPSET?**

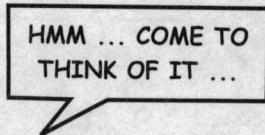

> HMM ... COME TO THINK OF IT ...

Many people who have been hurt as children remain locked into that **WOUNDED CHILD** without realising it.

> LET'S SORT IT OUT!

Would a **TRUE ADULT** respond in the ways described above?

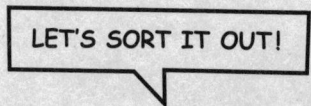

THE ADULT PERSPECTIVE:

MY LIFE, MY CHOICES!

It's up to **ME** to decide what I do with **MY LIFE**.

I'M OK!

YOU'RE OK!

I attract people who reflect my own **SENSE OF WORTH** ...

EEK!

... But I don't have to like **EVERYONE** and not everyone has to like **ME**.

Working things through **EMPOWERS** me. Running away **WEAKENS** me.

I set clear **BOUNDARIES** about what I am willing to take on board.

I am not **OBLIGED** to do anything I am not **COMFORTABLE** with.

~~HAVE TO~~
~~GOT TO~~
~~MUST~~

I recognise and **RESPECT** that others have different views from mine.

IT'S WHAT YOU DO ...

... NOT WHO YOU ARE!

I can **DISAGREE** with someone and still see the **GOOD** in them.

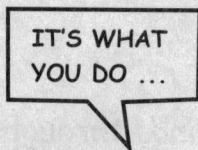

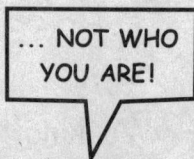

THE CHILD'S PERSPECTIVE:

Things just **HAPPEN** to me that are beyond my **CONTROL**.

If I don't **PLEASE** everyone, I will be **ABANDONED**.

NOTHING NOWHERE NO ONE

BAD!

It must be **MY FAULT** if **BAD THINGS** happen.

I can't **HELP** what I do.

131

LONELY SAD
CALM SICK
ANGRY HAPPY

People/things **MAKE ME** feel a certain way.

YOU'RE TIRED! GO TO BED!

I don't know what **I WANT**. I need to be **TOLD**.

If I am **MYSELF** I won't be **LOVED**.

EVERYTHING is horrible. I can't **COPE**.

Can you feel how **SCARED** that small person in you is?

How **POWERLESS** he or she feels?

There is no point in **TERRORISING** him or her any further. He or she feels **HELPLESS** enough as it is. That child needs your **NURTURE** and **CALM DIRECTION**. He or she needs to feel **SAFE**.

Let the **ADULT SELF** step up and **STAND BY** that small hurt part of you. The last thing you need is more **HARSHNESS**, **HORROR STORIES** or **PUNISHMENT**.

STOP SCARING THE CHILD!

NURTURE YOUR INNER CHILD

Talk **GENTLY** to yourself

ALL IS WELL!

OK, HOW LIKELY IS THAT?

Rationalise your **FEARS**

Reconnect with your **PLAYFULNESS**

TIME FOR SOME R & R

ARE YOU TELLING ME SOMETHING?

and
Respond immediately to your **BODY**'s needs.

Too often we **PUT OFF** even the basics of self-care.

Through learning to respond to your **BODY**'s and **MIND**'s needs **AS THEY ARISE**, you not only begin to **IDENTIFY** and **ACCOMMODATE** these needs more readily but your **BODY/MIND** doesn't have to get to the point of **SCREAMING** at you before you look after it!

This doesn't just apply to **PHYSICAL NEEDS**! **EMOTIONAL NEEDS** require attention too ...

... otherwise, you end up with an **EMOTIONAL STOCKPILE**!

In being attuned to your needs and making your self-care a **PRIORITY**, you help the wounded **CHILD** within feel much more **SECURE** in the knowledge that you are **LOOKING OUT** for him or her.

Now, go and find a picture of yourself when you were a child.

Take a good look at the **SMALL PERSON** you were.

INNOCENT AND OPEN

JUST WANTS TO BE LOVED

PLAYFUL AND INQUISITIVE

TRUSTING HEART

KEEN TO LEARN

FORGIVING

SMALL VUNERABLE BODY

LOOKS UP TO PEOPLE

How can that little person have **DESERVED** anything **BAD**? Reclaim your **INNOCENCE**. It wasn't **YOUR FAULT!**

You could only do what you **KNEW** how to do according to what you were **TAUGHT**. You coped as well as you could with life's challenges given the **TOOLS** that you had.

YOU DID THE BEST YOU COULD!

And guess what?

HEY, I'M STILL STANDING!

You're still here, you're still going, you're still trying, despite all that life has thrown at you.

Well done, you! You're **WORTH THE BEST**!

So, from here on, **YOU** need to be your own:

CHEER SQUAD

COMFORTER

ADVISER

NURTURER

and **BEST FRIEND**!

Because then you'll **ALWAYS** have someone to **TURN TO**!

FALLING IN LOVE WITH YOURSELF

LET'S DANCE!

Act as if you **ALREADY ARE!**

SHOW others how you want to be **TREATED**

RESPECT

DUDE
IDIOT
STUPID

Refuse to **PUT YOURSELF DOWN**

Choose **FUN** over **MISERY**

PIARY
STAY
HOME
BE
SAD

DIARY
GO OUT
FEEL
BETTER

and, above all, **GIVE YOURSELF** all that you would want someone else to give you.

That way, you don't need to **WAIT** for it to come to you!

The benefits of self-love

ME,

MYSELF

AND I

'You can search throughout the entire universe for someone who is more deserving of your love and affection than you are yourself, and that person is not to be found anywhere. You yourself, as much as anybody in the entire universe, deserve your love and affection.'

Buddha

So, how **HEALTHY** is your current relationship with yourself?

Let's take a look at how we might define **LOVE** and how that also translates into **SELF-LOVE**.

LOVE:	SELF-LOVE:
Compassion	Compassion for self
Caring	Self-nurturing
Acceptance	Maintaining energy and optimism
Respect	Setting clear boundaries
Tolerance	Accepting own shortfalls
Gentleness	Being kind to self
Forgiveness	Forgiving self through learning from mistakes
Helping others	Listening to own needs

To create a more loving relationship with yourself it is important that you build a better **CONNECTION** with yourself and thus take better **CARE** of yourself.

It may seem a little **TRITE** to simply point out that taking care of yourself involves such things as:

EATING WELL

GETTING ENOUGH
REST

EXERCISING   and   BEING HAPPY

because, let's face it, people who **LOVE THEMSELVES** do these things anyway and people who **LOVE THEMSELVES** probably don't need a book telling them **HOW TO**!

It might be more helpful at this point to go back to the quote by Epictetus at the very start of this book:

'GOD HAS ENTRUSTED ME WITH MYSELF'

<u>F.Y.I.</u> Epictetus was born into slavery about 55 CE in the eastern outreaches of the Roman Empire. Once freed, he established a school of philosophy, stressing that human beings cannot control life, only their responses to it.

Whatever your thoughts may be about God or religion the message in this quote is a powerful reminder that you are a **GIFT** to yourself.

You have been given this **PACKAGE** to work with: this **MIND**, **BODY** and **SPIRIT**.

I'VE ARRIVED!

These are the precious **RAW MATERIALS** you came into this world with.

They were **UNIQUE** and **PERFECTLY SUITED** to whatever you decided to use them for.

EARTH
MISSION
DISCOVER
SELF
LOVE

WELL, I'M GOING TO EXPLORE SELF-LOATHING FIRST!

And you were free to make of them **ANYTHING** you liked.

You and you alone are the **CARETAKER** and **GUARDIAN** of the gift that is you. How do you **TREAT** this gift?

Do you:

KEEP IT INTACT?

NOT ALLOW OTHERS TO TAMPER WITH IT?

LOOK AFTER ITS MAINTENANCE?

PROTECT IT FROM DESTRUCTIVE ELEMENTS?

KEEP IT IN PLEASANT SURROUNDINGS?

ENSURE THAT IT IS BRIGHT AND SHINY?

145

ENJOY
HAVING IT?

and
APPRECIATE IT?

You are ALL you have!

You are
EVERYTHING!

And you are **VERY, VERY POWERFUL** because:

If you **BELIEVE** you're **GREAT** ...

I'M PROUD TO BE ME!

you **ARE**!

How **POWERFUL** is that??

LOVING YOURSELF means you:

CHOOSE the best

A1 QUALITY

EXPECT the best

SORRY, IT'S NOT OK WITH ME.

Refuse to be **COMPROMISED**

Don't fear others' **DISAPPROVAL** because you like who you are

Don't need to be **DEFENSIVE**, because you don't fear attack

Feel **EQUAL** to others rather than superior or inferior

Have **COMPASSION** for self and others

Are **INDEPENDENT**

Are strong enough to be **TRUTHFUL**

MY BODY WORKS
BETTER ON
GOOD FOOD!

Make healthy
CHOICES

and
When you love yourself
you wouldn't **DREAM**
of making yourself
UNHAPPY, ANXIOUS,
UPSET, or **LONELY** or
talking to yourself in a
CRITICAL, HARSH OR
HOSTILE way!

WHY WOULD I DO
THAT TO MYSELF?
I'D MUCH RATHER
FEEL GOOD!

Everything is
INTERCONNECTED.

And, through your very **EXISTENCE**, you
play a **VITAL** role in the scheme of things.

The world simply would not be the same
WITHOUT YOU!

HISTORY OF EVERYTHING

HANG ON! WE'RE MISSING SOMEONE!

Realise that to get to **HERE**, you had to be **THERE** first, and, to move on to the **NEXT THING**, you need to go through this **CURRENT EXPERIENCE**.

It's all part of the **PROCESS**!

I GET IT! I COULD ONLY LOVE MYSELF BY DISCOVERING IT DIDN'T FEEL GOOD *HATING MYSELF!*

Your experience of **LIFE** is made up
entirely of the **CHOICES** you make.

You **COULD** choose to be **HAPPY** with
WHO YOU ARE and **WHERE YOU ARE**,
NO MATTER WHAT, and see what things
look like from that perspective ...

And who knows?
You just may discover you were **PERFECT**
all along!

OTHER BOOKS BY BEV AISBETT

Taming the Black Dog

Don't want to get out of bed in the morning?
Feeling as though the light at the end of the tunnel
is fading? You may be suffering from depression,
a condition Winston Churchill referred to as the
Black Dog.

Taming the Black Dog is a simple guide to managing
depression, which an estimated 1 in 5 people will
suffer in one form or another at some time in their
lives. This small, illustrated tip book contains factual
information as well as treatment options.

Modelled on Bev Aisbett's successful *Living with
IT*, *Taming the Black Dog* has a unique blend of wit
and information and is an invaluable guide for both
chronic sufferers of depression and anyone with a fit
of 'the blues'.

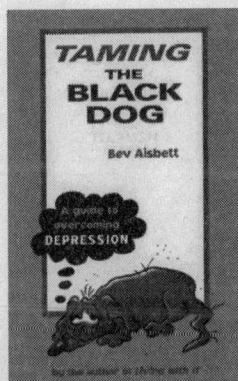

The Book of IT

Do you beat yourself up over mistakes?
Do you often worry, worry, worry?
Do you tend to expect the worst?
Do things have to be perfect before you can enjoy them?
Do you have a belief that life is hard?
Are you overly concerned about what others think of you?
Do you compare yourself to others?
Do you find it hard expressing your feelings, especially anger?
Do you give more than you get?
Do you look after others more than you do yourself?
Are you critical of yourself and others?
If you answered 'yes' to even half of these questions, would you say that your life and emotions are in balance?

Anxiety isn't a punishment — it's a wake-up call, and you can do something about it!

Using 10 steps from her popular workshops, counsellor Bev Aisbett provides you with practical, sound advice on how to recognise and tame anxiety, whether it affects you just occasionally or every single day.

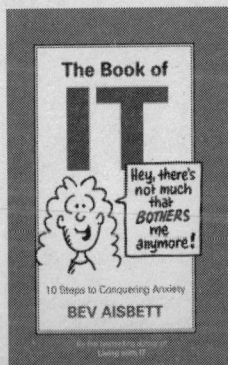

The Book of

IT

Hey, there's not much that *BOTHERS* me anymore!

10 Steps to Conquering Anxiety

BEV AISBETT

Letting IT Go

As a survivor of Panic Disorder, Bev Aisbett had a lot to live with. But she overcame IT and has shared with us the secrets of her success in several bestselling books.

In *Letting IT Go*, Bev Aisbett shows us how we can use the strategies she learned in her journey of self-discovery to achieve change and growth in our lives. Now Bev Aisbett has a lot to live for. And we can too!

- recognise self-limiting beliefs
- improve our self-esteem
- change our negative attitudes
- benefit from fortuitous coincidences in our lives
- improve our intimate relationships and ourselves
- learn to love and forgive others and ourselves